Hack Music Theory

Part 1: Learn scales & chords in 30 minutes

Ray Harmony

"The most brilliant, fast, easy, and fun music theory book I've ever seen!"
 –DEREK SIVERS, CD Baby founder, TED speaker, musician, author of
 Anything You Want: 40 Lessons for a New Kind of Entrepreneur

"This is the kind of book I wish I had when I first started out – a book that straightaway emphasises the simplicity of how these twelve notes are connected, rather than presenting every scale and interval as a separate mystery."
 –IHSAHN, Emperor

"Ray has his own unique style of teaching. His methods are fun and always bring music theory to life for me. Trust Ray, and in no time you'll have a watertight music theory skillset you once thought impossible to obtain."
 –PAT LUNDY, Modestep, ex-Funeral for a Friend

"Ray Harmony, making music theory punk since 1979. Going from Grade 0 to Grade 8, the highest grade, in a year seemed like an impossible task; however, after my very first lesson I was truly blown away. Ray manages to make learning music theory fascinating, digestible, and damn right cool! He opened my eyes and ears to a whole new world of music, and did so in an artistic and creative way that I'll never forget."
 –JOE COPCUTT, AxeWound, Zoax

"There is beauty in simplicity, and an art to making complexity seem simple. In *Hack Music Theory*, Ray Harmony gifts us a personal guided tour around the foundation principles of western tonal music. This book would be of particular interest to adults who are undertaking music education after a long break or perhaps for the first time. The explanations are accessible and the 'hacks' take advantage of memorable visuals. If you have been put off music theory in the past, then this is the book to inspire and empower you."
 –VICTORIA WILLIAMSON, PhD, Vice Chancellor's Fellow Researcher and
 Lecturer in Music at the University of Sheffield, UK, author of
 You Are the Music: How Music Reveals What it Means to Be Human

"Ray has a totally unique approach of hacking music theory, which gives you the essentials in a fraction of the time."
 –VESPERS, Warp Academy founder, music producer

ABOUT THE AUTHOR

Ray Harmony in his natural habitat.

My name's Ray Harmony (né Holroyd), and I've dedicated my life to using the power of music to inspire positive change in the world, which I do through Revolution Harmony. I'm a British African based in Canada, and an award-winning music lecturer, composer, performer, producer, and journalist, as well as a few other things, too.

I've been studying music for over thirty years, and teaching it for over twenty. My first No. 1 single was back in 1996 in my birth country of South Africa, and during the last few years in Canada I've been making music with multiplatinum Grammy-winning artists (Tom Morello of Rage Against the Machine, Serj Tankian of System of a Down, and many more), then donating all the proceeds to charities that restore harmony between people, animals, and the environment.

Between my time in South Africa and Canada, I immigrated to England where I spent a decade (2001–2011) lecturing music theory and composition at Ealing, Hammersmith and West London College, one of Europe's largest colleges. I was also the course director and lead internal verifier for the music department, and was honoured to win EHWLC's prestigious Vocational Qualification Hero and Learner First awards.

My education is a unique blend of 'classical' from the UK's Royal Schools of

Music (piano, guitar, and theory, all to the highest grade) and 'contemporary' from the USA's Musicians Institute in Los Angeles, where I graduated from their guitar program. I studied education and did my teaching qualification at EHWL College in London.

I've been writing for various publications (Kerrang!, Terrorizer, and more) every month since 2009, and I used to be the editor of a guitar magazine as well, until I once again moved countries. I've run a couple of record labels, too, but nowadays I spend all my time making music, teaching music, and writing about music.

Learn more at HackMusicTheory.com
Come say hello at RayHarmony.com

This book is dedicated to all my past, present, and future students.

TABLE OF CONTENTS

Hack Music Theory

Part 1: Learn scales & chords in 30 minutes

HOW TO USE THIS BOOK

Wanna learn Music Theory in 30 minutes?

No prob! Each chapter is preceded by a hack (i.e. a cheat sheet) that delivers all the vital info you need to know about that topic. Read through all the hacks in 30 minutes or less, ignoring the full chapters, and you're good to go. You'll miss out on a bunch of bad jokes and deep insights, but you'll be making good music in less than an hour from now.

Oh yeah, one more thing. To keep you skipping merrily along, I've added a handy glossary for quick reference. All terms in bold have their definitions waiting patiently for you in the back. And it goes without saying, which is silly cos now I'm gonna say it, but the debut of a term will always have its explanation with it. However, later in the book if you come across a term you know was mentioned earlier but now looks Greek, please use the glossary. Unless it's Pythagoras, he looks Greek cos he is Greek.

Wanna learn more about why and how music works?

Great! Read this book cover to cover, then use the hacks as references afterwards.

Important tips

Music is sound and hearing is believing, so try playing the examples in this book on a piano app, a virtual piano online, or a real piano if you're old-school. Doing this or not doing this won't affect your understanding of the content, but hearing it all come to life sure is fun.

Also, you definitely don't need to read this book in one sitting, though you easily could. Please remember, however, that understanding music theory is an accumulative action, so you'll probably have questions at the end of each chapter that will be answered in subsequent chapters. And, just like in a murder mystery where you have to get to the end before the whole picture becomes clear, our music theory story is still unfolding, too. All shall be revealed soon, so keep reading!

Lastly, you'll get the best results from reading this book cover to cover, and then repeating that until it's all soaked in. I've been told that using the book as a pillow while you're sleeping also helps this osmosis. (Disclaimer: please don't sue me if you sleep on your e-reader and the screen cracks.)

HELLO

Musical harmony has the power to improve personal harmony, mindfulness, health, and connections, and can even fuel revolutions towards a societal harmony. Power to the people, and that power is music!

Growing up in apartheid South Africa, I was surrounded by people of all colours united through music, and only through music. Heroic bands like the multiracial National Wake and – my personal favourites – South African singers Lucky Dube and Johnny Clegg, created the pot of gold out of which Nelson Mandela would later build the Rainbow Nation. Most inspiringly, they did this in the 1970s and 1980s, right under the nose of the apartheid regime. Music is invisible and can be orally shared, making it impossible to confiscate or suppress. We can feel music but we can't touch it, and if that's not the best party trick ever, I don't know what is! Black and white together in harmony, like the keyboard of a piano: that was my introduction to the power of music and why I believe access to music education should be a human right.

Movement causes vibration, and vibration causes sound, which is why on an astronomic level the planets are making 'music of the spheres,' and on a microscopic level our bodies are making 'cell symphonies.' We are music, literally. Every culture we know of uses music to enhance life and unite people. Before the days of recording, there was a far larger percentage of musicians, because if you wanted to listen to music you had to play it yourself. When it became possible to capture songs and sell them as products, a tectonic shift forced musicians above everyone else with the implication that they have something unique, which is why they're on the record and you're not. However, in reality we're all born with the capacity to communicate through music: we just have to understand the language. Everyone, and I do mean everyone, can learn music. There are really no reasons not to learn music, and countless reasons to learn it. You don't even need to have an instrument, as most music in this digital age is produced on computers. In fact, I composed and recorded the music for my all-star charity single 'Hello,' featuring Tom Morello (Rage Against the Machine) and friends, on a laptop in my living room, using nothing more than REAPER digital audio workstation ($60) and virtual instruments, some of which are even available for free.

On a planet with over seven billion humans, music is our only shared language, and harmony is our only hope. By learning the language of music, also known as music theory, you can create harmony in your life and your community. Thank you for having the courage and commitment to make the world a better place through music. Together we are all the Revolution Harmony. Amandla Awethu!

PREFACE

Theory! Scary, huh? As a music lecturer, I discovered that this six-letter 'dirty word' always caused an impressive array of strong reactions from my new first-year students. No other word can end the party quicker than this one. Students react in a variety of ways to this word: first, there are the flinchers, who physically tense up – often with the addition of lip curling that even the most potent salt and vinegar chips can't induce. Then there are the sighers, who would make great trumpet players with their huge cheeks and lungs, often including eye-rolling for extra emphasis. Then there are the pee-ers, who suddenly have full bladders and need to be excused for lengthy toilet breaks, even though it's only two minutes into the first lecture of the day. Finally, there's the nerd – yes, just the one – who perks up and aims their pen at that blank 300-page notebook, ready for action. Don't get me wrong, nerds are awesome – but this is a book for the flinchers, the sighers, and the pee-ers. This is a book for us, the 99%.

Please stop reading for a moment. No, not yet, that was too soon. Okay, please stop reading after this sentence and take a few seconds to scan your body. Scanning, scanning, scanning. Finished? Good. If you found your shoulders tense and your lips curled, then read on. If you found your cheeks puffed out and your eyes wandering, then read on. And, of course, if you found yourself spontaneously in the bathroom with nothing to do, then definitely read on. However, if you belong to the perky 1%, then you're probably better off reading the classic *AB Guide to Music Theory* from the Associated Board of the Royal Schools of Music.

We've now established that we're all in the right place. Welcome to a better future! A future that will find you happy, healthy, successful, rich, and – obviously – famous. Erm… theory can and absolutely will make all of these a reality, probably… well, maybe… actually, maybe not. Fine, my book isn't going to do any of those things for you. But it kept you reading, didn't it? That's my mission, to keep you reading and learning, and hopefully also entertained along the journey. By the time we reach our destination of the final book in this series, you'll have the knowledge to figure out why your favourite song is so powerful, and, better yet, you'll actually be able to compose your new favourite song yourself, even if you don't play an instrument – that's what computers are for. Also, if you need an internationally-recognised qualification, or just want to be the proud owner of a shiny music certificate, you'll have the level of education needed to write the London College of Music's highest grade Popular Music Theory exam, which is held worldwide. So while I can't help you diminish debt, I can help you understand what a diminished fifth interval is and amaze you with the story of why it was banned from music, all while helping you become qualified.

I'll be honest with you. Theory is a six-letter dirty word to most musicians, but, hey, musicians love dirty words, right? And just like all the other dirty words, theory is easy to learn and fun to use! See what I did there? No? Confused? Well, this is the last time you'll be confused when it comes to theory, as here's my promise to you: using my two decades of music teaching and industry experience, combined with my minimalist methods of explaining, I'll break down music theory into its simplest form and then show it to you using the simplest way possible, all via a series of simple chapters and even simpler hacks. I'll start at the very beginning, so you don't need any prior theory experience. Just bring your love of music and I'll bring everything else. Remember, theory is music, and music is fun. Enjoy this! Besides, contrary to what music snobs would like you to believe, theory really is easy, as there are a mere twelve notes in all music. Every element of theory has been used to write songs, and every song has theory behind it, so let's go backstage and get behind the scenes to find out how it all works. Right, please follow me…

1. PITCH & RHYTHM

There are only ever two ingredients that make up all music: pitch and rhythm.

Rhythm is a *pattern in time.**

Pitch is the *frequency of vibrations, resulting in the highness or lowness of a sound, aka a* **note**. It can be expressed in **melody** (horizontal) – a *sequence of notes sounded one at a time*, or in **harmony** (vertical) – *two or more notes sounded together*, or in both.

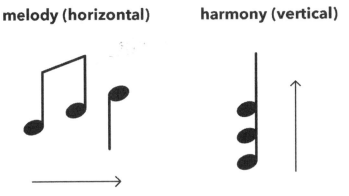

Figure 1.1 Music notation showing the horizontal movement of an unfolding melody, versus the simultaneous vertical stacking of notes to form harmony (e.g. a **chord**, *three or more notes sounded together*).

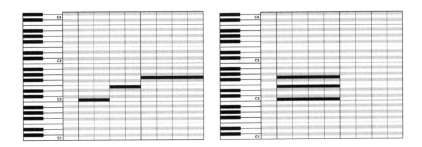

Figure 1.2 MIDI notation in a digital audio workstation's piano roll, showing melody (left) versus harmony (right)

*Rhythm is independent of **tempo**, or the *speed at which music is played*. A rhythm can be played fast, slow, or somewhere in between, but it's all still the same rhythm.

If music is a painting, then theory is the paint. You can't have one without the other. Paint combined with imagination creates good artwork, and theory combined with imagination creates good songs. Unlike in art, however, we musicians only have two 'colours' to work with. Every song we make, no matter how complicated, is nothing more than various shades and combinations of these two 'colours'. What are they? Drum roll please... pitch and rhythm!

Rhythm

This is where it probably all began, though musicologists are still arguing over the origins of music and which came first, pitch or rhythm. While the precise beginnings of our art may be uncertain, what isn't uncertain is the importance of rhythm. This is the magic ingredient that gets our feet tapping and heads bopping – the element of music that literally moves us. Rhythm has been around for thousands of years and we instinctively know what it is, but ask someone to define it and you'd think it was invented yesterday. How can something so simple be so difficult to describe? I think it's because rhythm is built into our DNA: our hearts start playing our inner rhythm before we're even born and continue to play our personal soundtracks throughout our lives. Rhythm is to music what our heartbeat is to our body. It's absolutely vital, but it's not something we tend to think about. Therefore, we often take it for granted and don't discuss it as much as we do pitch. This is a real shame, and often results in rhythm becoming an afterthought in music, whereas it could and should be as integral as the pitches it's attached to. Finally, here is the simplest way to define the elusive term: **rhythm** is a *pattern in time*. Now go forth and play with time. Clap the rhythms you hear in nature or on TV and have fun creating new patterns for old songs or using old rhythmic ideas in a fresh setting.

Pitch

Pitch is the element of music that's determined by the *frequency of vibrations, resulting in the highness or lowness of a sound, aka a* **note**. Pitch can be divided into melody and harmony. **Melody** is also known as the tune, or, if you prefer a more standard definition, a *sequence of notes sounded one at a time*. **Harmony**, on the other hand, is when *two or more notes are sounded together*; this is known as a **chord** when there are *three or more notes sounded together*. We visualise melody as horizontal music, because it moves along one note at a time, and harmony as vertical music, because the notes are all on top of each other. I love harmony, as it's the one-and-only aspect of music that doesn't require time to reveal itself. Both melody and rhythm, like stories, take seconds and minutes to unfold. Harmony is like visual art: you see it all at once and that 'wall of sound' can hit you with such power it'll take your breath away. Thankfully, though, as our late friend Bob Marley famously mused: "One good thing about music, when it hits you, you feel no pain." So go on, sing a song to enjoy a melody or two, then get a friend to join in to savour some harmony.

melody (horizontal)   harmony (vertical)

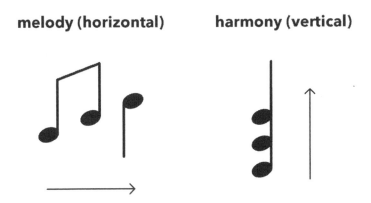

2. NOTES & ENHARMONICS

This is your alphabet, literally and musically. The first seven letters of our English alphabet are used for the *white notes on a piano*, aka **naturals**, and for the five black notes we just add sharps (♯) or flats (♭) to those first seven letters. All music is made from just these twelve notes – it's that simple!

Sharp (♯) *1 step up* (e.g. C♯ is 1 step* up from C)

Flat (♭) *1 step down* (e.g. D♭ is 1 step down from D)

Enharmonic is a *different name for the same note* (e.g. C♯ and D♭ are enharmonics).

When you count through all twelve steps (i.e. notes) and end up on the same letter again, that's known as an **octave**: *same note, but a higher or lower pitched version.*

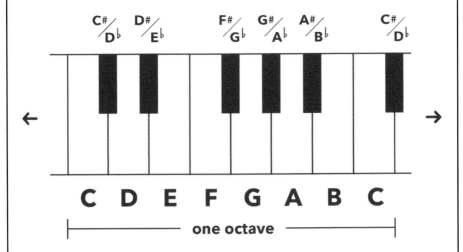

Figure 2.1 Notes on a piano keyboard

***Step** is not a musical term, and is therefore ambiguous. We will upgrade this with an unambiguous musical term in the following two hacks.*

Notes

You already know that in music we have fewer 'colours' than in art, and now I have more good news for you. We also have fewer 'letters' than in the English alphabet. We only use the first seven letters of that alphabet (A through G) for our musical notes. These seven letters are the white notes on a piano. If you look at a piano keyboard, you'll see seven white notes that repeat themselves in the same shape, along with five black notes within that shape. The first white note in this group is C, and if we move up/right or down/left through this twelve-step cycle (seven white notes and five black notes), we arrive at another C – this time a higher or lower pitched one, respectively. When we play the same note twelve steps above or below, it's called an **octave**. The word 'octave' comes from the Greek word *oktō*, meaning eight, as there are eight letters (notes) in an octave, including the repeated starting note: C D E F G A B C. This is why the octave is sometimes referred to as the 8th. If you're interested in science, you'll be fascinated to know that the sound wave of a note an octave higher will vibrate at twice the frequency, and if we play it down an octave the wave will vibrate at half the frequency. The faster the vibration the higher the pitch, and the slower the vibration the lower the pitch. The piano is a great instrument when it comes to visualising theory, as the notes are different colours, which makes everything so easy it's like an honest form of cheating. There are a few rare exceptions that we'll get to later, but generally speaking the *white notes on a piano* are known as **naturals**, and the black notes are known as sharps or flats. A **sharp** (♯) note is *1 step up* from its original, and a **flat** (♭) note is *1 step down* from its original.

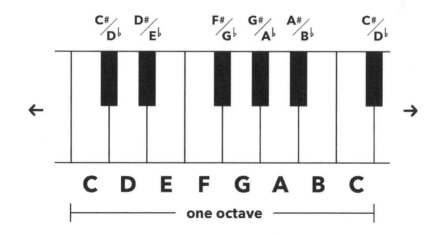

Enharmonics

Want to impress some friends with your new theory knowledge? Next time you're out enjoying a fine tea and some good conversation, tell them you'd like to discuss enharmonics. Or perhaps if you're being asked to wash the dishes after dinner, shout "Enharmonic!" and run. That'll confuse 'em and should buy you some time. Although this fancy word will both impress and irritate those bewildered non-theory-knowing people around you, it's actually such a ridiculously basic concept to understand that you must never reveal its true meaning to the outsiders. Now, an **enharmonic** is a *different name for the same note.* You wanted something grander, I know. Sorry to disappoint, but, like everything in music, it's simple and easy. Let me give you an example of an enharmonic. You've already learnt that if we move one step up from C we land on C♯, and if we move one step down from D we land on D♭, which makes C♯ and D♭ enharmonic equivalents: same note, different name. Depending on its surroundings, this note will either be a C♯ or a D♭, but it can only ever have one name within each context. So, yes, sometimes calling a C♯ a D♭ is actually incorrect, even though you're describing the same note. More on this intriguing topic in chapter 7.

3. TUNING

Tuning* means two things. First, we tune our instruments and voices in order to play and sing the correct pitches. Second, it's the precise pitch of each note that we tune our instruments and voices to that makes up our tuning system.

We use a system known as equal temperament to tune all our musical instruments in the west. Whether you're working with a keyboard, guitar, voice, MIDI sequencer, or any other instrument, you're already experiencing this tuning system.

Equal temperament *divides the octave into twelve equal steps*, known as semitones. A **semitone** is the *smallest space between notes in western music, and is a distance of one step*. This mathematical averaging actually pushes our new musical notes slightly out of tune from where Mother Nature placed them and Pythagoras discovered them.

Just intonation is the *original 'pure' tuning system that uses whole-number ratios, and works only from one fundamental note at a time*. This was fine for simple medieval music, but just intonation simply doesn't cut it anymore, as nowadays we demand freedom to musically travel to any note, any chord, any time!

Advantage of equal temperament: We can play any chords, without having to retune.

Disadvantage of equal temperament: Our music is a tiny bit out of tune.

---

*Tuning is one of the most fascinating yet complicated musical (not theoretical) topics, which is why I've included it. If you wanna push on with the theory though, feel free to skip this hack as it's pretty much just backstory. Besides, a lot of pro musicians don't even know this stuff!

All the music we listen to is out of tune! Seriously. I'm afraid that's a scientific fact, which makes this subject another conversation starter, or stopper, depending on your company. Don't worry, this isn't where music theory becomes conspiracy theory, and please don't delete all your music in protest, as none of those songs would even exist unless they were all a little out of tune. Let me explain – but first, what is tuning? Tuning means two things. First, we tune our instruments and voices in order to play and sing the correct pitches. Second, it's the precise pitch of each note that we tune our instruments and voices to that makes up our tuning system.

Our musical notes have been extracted from nature, and, more specifically, from the harmonic series. Just like throwing a pebble into a pond causes ripples, whenever a note is sounded its vibrations also ripple out and set off a series of higher notes, which perform as backing vocalists and sing softly along. The **harmonic series** is the *series of higher notes that are set off from the vibrations of a single note*. If you've ever heard overtone singers, like the Gyuto Monks of Tibet, then you're already familiar with this phenomenon. We refer to all these *quieter notes that occur in the harmonic series* as **overtones**, and they make up the harmonic series. If you want to get fancy, overtones' wavelengths can be mathematically explained as whole-number ratios (e.g. 2:1) of the low fundamental note. For example, if you pluck two strings of the same thickness and tension, where the second string is half the length of the first, for every single sound wave vibration of the long string, the short one vibrates twice, producing a note that's an octave higher. This *original 'pure' tuning system that uses whole-number ratios, and works only from one fundamental note at a time*, is called **just intonation**. By the way, the amazingness of overtone singers is that they've learnt how to turn up their inner 'backing vocalists,' so you can hear the low, or fundamental, note they're singing along with these higher rippled notes (overtones) as well. Harmony from one voice. Amazing!

Until the late Renaissance, composers would mostly make simple music that stuck both to one fundamental pitch and to a few notes from its harmonic series, which the old just intonation tuning was perfect for. The majority of music was also vocal, another way to sidestep the hassle of constantly retuning instruments to different fundamentals. However, the tidal wave that 15th century British composer John Dunstaple had started with his complex music eventually swelled into a widespread demand for full creative liberation that just intonation couldn't provide due to its fundamental limitations. As composers became more interested in musical travel to any and all notes, the need for a tuning system that could provide this freedom became paramount. To put things into perspective, if they hadn't solved this problem back then, we'd now be trying to find ways for technology to somehow retune our instruments between every chord change. And, far worse than that, the vast majority of music that's been born in the last few centuries would've been impossible to create.

For over a millennium, great minds in both Asia and Europe had been working on the idea of *dividing the octave into twelve equal steps* (**equal temperament**), which would sever those shackles to a fundamental pitch and permit the migration of music to any note without the need to retune your instrument. The turning point finally came in 1722, when the genius J.S. Bach (my hero!) mastered a way of tuning his keyboard so he could play anything, anywhere, anytime. He celebrated this historic achievement by writing a collection of compositions that did exactly that, titled *The Well-Tempered Clavier*. Although there were countless people who all worked tirelessly over the years to make this dream a reality, it was Bach's music that took it to the world. By the 1830s, most instruments were being manufactured using the new tuning system, and this invention of dividing the octave into *twelve equal steps*, known as **semitones**, has gone on to revolutionise music by allowing everyone from Beethoven to the Beatles (and yes, even Bieber) to play music using all of the notes without retuning. The downside to this averaging of our pitches is that some of them are now slightly out of tune to what nature intended, but I'm sure you'll agree that the infinite upsides are more than worth it. (The octave can, of course, be divided into any number of steps, like in the Arabic musical system where they halve western semitones into quartertones, resulting in twenty-four notes to an octave. If you haven't heard music like this, do yourself a favour and listen to some, as it's utterly mesmerizing and magical.)

4. MAJOR SCALE

A **scale** is a *family of notes that work together*. The original family is the **major scale**, often referred to as the 'happy scale' due to its cheerful sound. All major scales are exactly the same scale, made up from exactly the same formula but starting on a different note. This formula is derived from playing all the white notes on a piano, beginning with C. Therefore, the major scale formula (counted in steps, aka semitones) is: *2 2 1 2 2 2 1*

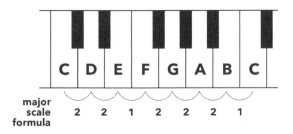

Figure 4.1 Major scale formula derived from white notes on a piano, starting on C

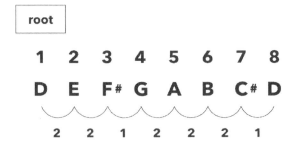

Figure 4.2 To find the D major scale, start the major scale formula on D

When writing out music, each note is assigned the number of its degree in the scale, from 1 to 7. We then use 8 to complete the scale and represent a version of the root an octave higher. This is called **spelling**, and is the *numerical way of writing music* (e.g. major scale = 1 2 3 4 5 6 7 8).

VOCAB EXTRAS
Root / root note / tonic *first note of a scale* (e.g. D is the root in D major)
Interval *space between any two notes, measured in semitones* (e.g. twelve semitones is the interval of an octave)
Semitone *smallest interval in western music and is an interval of one step* (e.g. C to C♯)
Tone / whole tone *interval of two semitones* (e.g. C to D)

As much as we love playing with notes, that's how much Pythagoras loved playing with numbers back in the good ol' BCE days. The Greek overachiever discovered that repeating a 3:2 frequency ratio (the next simplest after that ultra-pure 2:1 octave ratio) produced a pleasant sounding set of notes that he could make melodies from. This is further proof that music at its core is simple. The special notes are: C D E F G A B C. This would later become known as the **major scale**, or 'happy scale' due to its cheerful sound. Those notes probably look familiar too, as they're all the piano's white notes. Thanks to equal temperament tuning, we no longer need to calculate our scales using ratios. We simply use steps, aka semitones. As the piano keyboard is designed around C major, let's start there. By analysing the semitones between the white notes, we'll discover the underlying formula for all major scales. There are two steps (semitones) from C to D, as there's a black note in between, and there is one step (semitone) from E to F, and so on. Here is the complete major scale formula: *2 2 1 2 2 2 1*

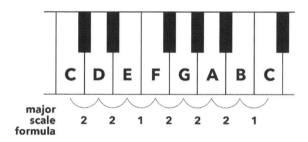

Now we can take this semitone sequence and start anywhere we want, like on D, for a D major scale:

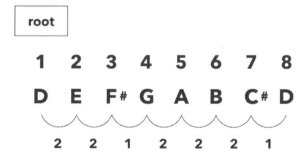

Finally, here's some more terminology to further impress your friends with. The *first note of a scale* is called its **root** or **root note**, or sometimes, **tonic**. An **interval** is the *space between any two notes, measured in semitones* (e.g. twelve semitones is the interval of an octave). The interval of one step is a **semitone**, and the *interval of two semitones* can be called a **tone**, or **whole tone**. The **spelling** of a scale or chord is the *numerical way of writing* it. Each note is assigned the number of its degree in the scale, from 1 to 7. We then use 8 to complete the scale and represent a version of the root an octave higher. The 1 and 8 are, of course, the same note, so technically a major scale only has seven different notes. Using numbers to represent the notes of a scale allows us to detach melodies and chords from specific pitches, revealing their underlying contours and shapes. This is one of the most vital concepts in understanding and composing music, as it gives you insight into your own preferences for certain musical patterns. And as a bonus, spelling music also enables you to move songs up or down in pitch, to better suit a singer's range. For example, if your melody started with the 1 followed by the 3, in C major, but you found that it was too low for your voice, you could move it up to D major and sing its 1 and 3 instead. The melodic contour and resulting emotion will be identical. However, if you referred to the notes in our C major melody as C and E (instead of 1 and 3), then you can't move them directly into D major. You'd first have to work out what degrees C and E are in C major, then take those numbers over to D major and work out the new notes. Numbers simplify music to the point of having only a single major scale. Rather than learning twelve different major scales – one for each note – we learn only one and apply its formula to whatever note we want to start from. So the next time you're walking down the street and someone asks you to spell a major scale, reply with 1 2 3 4 5 6 7 8 – and then run away as fast as you can, cos what kind of weirdo goes up to strangers and asks them to spell things?!

5. MINOR SCALE & RELATIVES

When you start on the 6th note of a major scale (the 'happy scale'), you get a **minor scale**, aka **natural minor scale** (nicknamed the 'sad scale'). By using one of the other notes within a scale as your root, you create different emotions without changing any notes.

For example, if you emphasise the 6th note in the C major scale as your root, you get the A minor scale. And vice versa: if you're in A minor and you want the major scale hiding within, emphasise the 3rd note (i.e. C) as your root. These two scales are **relatives**, or **relative scales**, as they are *scales that have the same notes, but a different root* (i.e. they start in a different place).

The **relative major** is *the scale you get when you start on the 3rd note of a minor scale.* The **relative minor** is *the scale you get when you start on the 6th note of a major scale.*

The formula for the natural minor scale is derived from playing all the white notes on a piano, starting on A. Counted in semitones, it is: *2 1 2 2 1 2 2*

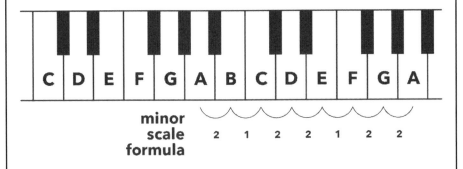

Figure 5.1 Minor scale, aka natural minor scale, formula derived from white notes, starting on A

VOCAB EXTRAS
Key the *scale in use* (e.g. a melody in the A minor scale is in the key of A minor)
Key signature the *sharps or flats in a scale* (e.g. F♯ and C♯ in D major – see Figure 4.2)

Music is life's sonic mirror, and life sure ain't rainbows and narwhals all the time (unless you're incredibly unlucky, as it's the difficult days that provide us with the best opportunities to learn and grow). When things are good, we have the major scale to express our happiness, but when the going gets tough, we need something stronger. No, not whiskey. We need a scale that can empathise with us in our darker moments, allowing for reflection and then progression. Please meet the **minor scale**, also known as the **natural minor scale**.

Following the birth of the major scale, an unexpected twin popped out: the minor. From making music using the major scale, it was discovered that the cheerful emotion could be completely flipped by merely accentuating the 6th note of that scale as the root. On a piano, if you play the C major scale with your right hand while your left hand plays a low C note, you get that 'happy' major vibe. However, if you play the same C major scale with your right hand, but this time your left hand plays a low A (the 6th note in C major), you get an entirely different atmosphere, a sad and sombre one. You've just turned C major into A minor, without changing any notes. Take that, David Copperfield! This trick also works the other way around. If you're playing in A minor and want to turn it major, simply emphasise the 3rd note (i.e. C) as the root and suddenly you're in C major, without changing a note. Like identical twins, these two scales share the same DNA but have totally different personalities, and that's why they're called **relatives**, or **relative scales**. These *scales have exactly the same notes, but a different root* (i.e. they start in a different place). As time went by, the minor scale underwent a couple of tweaks (we'll get to 'em later), which resulted in the original version becoming known as the natural minor scale in order to differentiate it from its variations. To conclude, when you count the semitones between each white note on a piano, starting from A, you get the natural minor scale formula: *2 1 2 2 1 2 2*

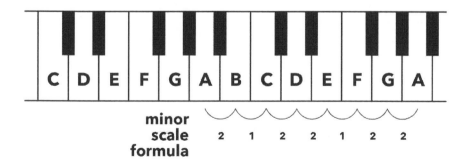

Now it's time to add some more terms to your music vocabulary, and, as always, I encourage you to insert them into your everyday conversations to annoy people. First up we have **key**, which refers to the *scale in use*. If you're composing a song and you make the intro using A minor, you'll say that intro is in the key of A minor. Next we have **key signature**, which is the *sharps or flats in a scale*. So the key signature of D major (discussed in the previous chapter) is F♯ and C♯. This will be helpful later…

Last, can we please take a moment to marvel at the life lesson that music is teaching us through relative keys? You can interpret every situation from two contrasting views: positive or negative. This always reminds me of my childhood, growing up ten minutes down the road from the Khayelitsha township in Cape Town. I'd see children there who couldn't even afford shoes, joyfully running around barefoot, truly happy and thankful to be alive. They're living a minor melody, but their choice to highlight the 3rd note turns everything to major. Then on the opposite extreme, many people in wealthy countries are living major melodies, but corporations work relentlessly to brainwash the masses via a bombardment of advertisements into focusing on the 6th note and feeling the relative minor. And, of course, the only way you can 'fix' your life is to buy their products. We can all learn a lot from music, and from the inspirational children of Khayelitsha. When life gives you a major scale, enjoy it with gratitude while sharing it, and when life gives you a minor scale, start on the 3rd!

6. FINDING RELATIVES

To find the relative minor, count three semitones *down* in pitch from the major scale root.

To find the relative major, count three semitones *up* in pitch from the minor scale root.

Remember, there is always a note (i.e. letter) skipped between the roots of relative scales, aka relative keys.

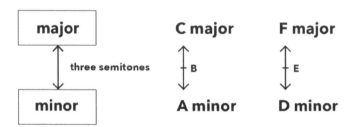

Figure 6.1 Shortcut to finding relative keys

Majors to relative minors (three semitones down)	Minors to relative majors (three semitones up)
B major = G♯ minor	D minor = F major
E♭ major = C minor	B♭ minor = D♭ major

Figure 6.2 Examples of relative keys

Have you seen the film *Finding Nemo*? Yeah, finding relatives isn't anything like that, but the fish are so cute, aren't they? Okay, back to work. If you're in a major key and want to find its relative minor, play the same scale but start on the 6th note. And, if you're in a minor key and want to find its relative major, play the same scale but start on the 3rd note. This method is great, but there's a much quicker way to find relatives, which will save you from having to first figure out the scale and only then count up. You know from the previous chapter that C major and A minor are relatives. The roots C and A are three semitones apart, and we can use this as a shortcut to find any relative. To find the relative minor, count three semitones down in pitch (e.g. C down to A). To find the relative major, count three semitones up in pitch (e.g. A up to C). The way I remember which direction to move is by thinking of the literal meanings of major as important and minor as less important. By these definitions, majors are above minors, so you would count down from a major to a minor, and up from a minor to a major.

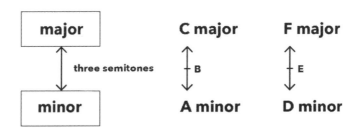

Let's practice this shortcut with an example. If we're in the key of E major, what is the relative minor? Take a minute to work it out, by counting three semitones down from E. Did you get D ♭ minor? If you did, congrats, you landed on the right note. But, as we can see from the original C major and A minor relatives, there is a note (i.e. letter) skipped – B – between their roots. Therefore, D ♭ minor can't be the relative of E major, as their roots are adjacent letters. Having said that, though, we're certain about the D ♭ as it's definitely three semitones down from E. This means we've got the correct note but the incorrect name for it. There's an easy solution to this problem that often arises. Whenever we know for sure that we're on the right note, but its name is wrong, we call on our

enharmonic friends. What's the enharmonic equivalent (other name) for D♭?
Yep, C♯. That means C♯ minor is the relative of E major. We haven't even
worked out the E major scale yet, but we already know its relative. That's a good
shortcut! Here are a few more examples to test out your new trick:

Majors to relative minors (three semitones down)	Minors to relative majors (three semitones up)
B major = G♯ minor	D minor = F major
E♭ major = C minor	B♭ minor = D♭ major

Remember, in order to properly switch into the relative, you need to emphasise
the new root, otherwise it'll sound like you're still in the same key. If I'm playing
in D minor and want to change to F major in order to lighten the emotion of my
song, it won't happen unless I actively make F sound more important than D.
There are numerous ways we can make a note sound prominent, like starting or
finishing the melody on it, or playing it longer or louder than the other notes. In
this D minor song, the instant our ears are drawn to F as the new home, we've
switched into the relative major and our mood will lift. Easy peasy.

7. WHY FLATS EXIST

Every major and minor scale must contain the first seven letters of the alphabet, otherwise things get confusing.

If you're working out a scale and you get to an A, and your formula says the next note is one semitone up (A♯), it must be referred to by its enharmonic (B♭), otherwise the scale will have two As and no B. This is the *sole reason for the existence of flats.*

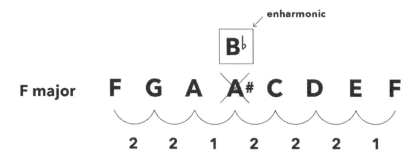

Figure 7.1 In F major, one semitone up from A must be referred to as B♭

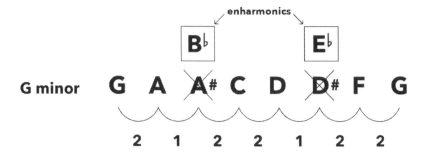

Figure 7.2 In G minor, we rename A♯ to B♭ and D♯ to E♭, in order for the scale to contain all seven letters

Remember, key signatures consist of *either sharps or flats*, not both.

A♯ and B♭ are two different names for the same note, so why don't we just call the note A♯ all the time? This is a great question, and provides me with the perfect opportunity to bust out another metaphor. When I was teaching at the college in London, we hired a new lecturer named Will, and all was well in the music department. Then we went on to hire another new lecturer, also named Will, and order descended into chaos within our music team. Will the Second decided to do the right thing and kindly volunteered himself for a name change to Bill. This was the only way we could avoid confusion, and it's exactly the same in music.

For example, when we work out the F major scale, we notice that the 3rd note is A and the 4th note is one semitone up from that (A♯). We now have two As in our team, which is thoroughly ambiguous, so we need to give the second A another name. Once again, enharmonics save the day. By using the other name for A♯ (i.e. B♭), everything is crystal clear when we're writing, reading, discussing, and playing music in F major. This is the *sole reason for the existence of flats*, and understanding this concept allows us to fully appreciate that having two names for each note doesn't make things more complicated – it actually prevents confusion and makes everything much simpler. I really dig how this also ensures that each note is treated equally, and while they're all connected and working together as a team, they're still individuals with individual names. How beautifully reflective of life and of a society living in harmony. This is why, depending on the context, it can be incorrect to refer to a note by its other name (as we mentioned in chapter 2), like in F major where there's no A♯, only B♭.

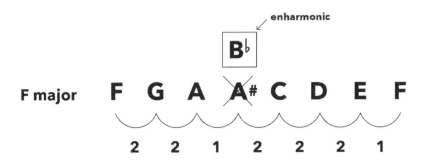

Let's do another one for practice, and let's try a minor this time. How about G minor? Take a few minutes to figure it out yourself, and, when you're done, have a look at my version and see if you got all the names correct for your new crew.

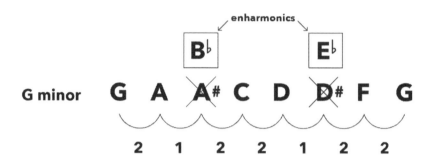

In G minor, we end up with two friends who need renaming. First, the A♯ is renamed B♭; second, the D♯ is renamed E♭. The key signature of G minor is therefore B♭ and E♭. It's worth noting that in both major and natural minor scales, you'll only ever have sharps or flats, never both. In other words, your key signatures consist of *either sharps or flats*. This will help keep you on the right path: if you're working out a major or natural minor scale and end up with both sharps and flats, then something must've gone wrong somewhere. Double-check the formula and count those intervals again. Now that everyone's here and happy with their names and individuality, we can continue respectfully, sans confusion.

8. DIFFERENCE BETWEEN MAJOR & MINOR SCALES

'Happy' major scales and 'sad' minor scales share four notes (1 2 4 5), while the other three notes (3 6 7) are different. The reason for these scales' opposite emotions must therefore lie within these three different notes.

The 3rd, 6th and 7th notes are *one semitone lower in natural minor scales than they are in major scales*. To represent this one semitone down, we add a flat (♭) to their spelling.

By their spelling, these flats tell us that their associated notes are one semitone down from where they are in a major scale. They don't tell us that the notes (i.e. letters) themselves are flats, like in A minor (below) where the ♭3 is C, a natural note.

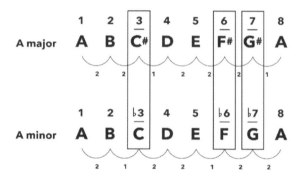

Figure 8.1 Comparison of A major scale to A natural minor scale

Major scale	1	2	**3**	4	5	**6**	**7**	8
Natural minor scale	1	2	♭**3**	4	5	♭**6**	♭**7**	8

Figure 8.2 Comparison of major and natural minor scale spellings

All major scales have the same underlying semitone formula and therefore the same spelling, and all natural minor scales have the same formula and spelling.

Remember, we write spellings and notes the way we say them. For example, flat three is written as ♭3 (sign before number), and F sharp is written as F♯ (sign after letter).

I know you've already read the title of this chapter and answered: Major scales sound happy and minor scales sound sad, done deal, next chapter please. You are correct, congrats! But before we move on, I'm going to briefly whisk you away on a nostalgic detour. Ready? Remember when we were kids, what our favourite follow-up question to every question we ever asked was? Of course, it was "why?" This one syllable would simultaneously empower our learning about the world while providing endless amusement as we watched adults squirm through 'explanations' of things they didn't understand themselves. Why is the sky blue? Why did Milli Vanilli win a Grammy for lip-syncing? Why does the paradox encountered in quantum entanglement work? You know, just the usual kid stuff. It's heartbreaking how our wonder dissolves into indifference as we grow older. I'll never forget the time many years ago when I stopped my car at a pedestrian crossing to let a father and son cross the road. As they walked in front of me I was struck by the shockingly vast divide between the adult and the child. The dad's gaze was firmly fixed on the ground with the weight of the world on his shoulders, while the child skipped along fuelled by inquisitiveness as he peered up at the infinite possibilities of the world. Please, let's regularly remind ourselves to reconnect with our inquisitive younger selves, as that's the most effective and fun way to learn and live.

I always make a deal with my students in their very first theory lesson: if they ever ask why something is the way it is or why it's relevant, and I can't explain, then they don't have to learn it. This keeps us all on our toes. Be warned, though: I've never lost. A little bragging about this fact always helps to motivate my students to be even more curious, if only to be able to say they beat me and claim the prize as the first person ever to win this challenge.

Now that you're in touch with your inner why-kid, I guess you're thinking: I can hear that majors are happy and minors are sad, but why? The best way to discover the differences between major and minor scales is to put them side by side and compare their notes. Let's do this with A major and A minor. As you can see below, there are four notes that are the same (1 2 4 5) and three notes that are different (3 6 7). The 3rd note in A major is C♯ and the 3rd note in A minor is C, which means the *3rd note in a minor scale is one semitone lower than the 3rd note in a major scale*. To show this we add a flat (♭), which represents one semitone down, to the spelling of the 3rd note in minor scales (i.e. ♭3). The same thing happens with the 6th and 7th notes in natural minor scales, as they're also one semitone lower than their major counterparts.

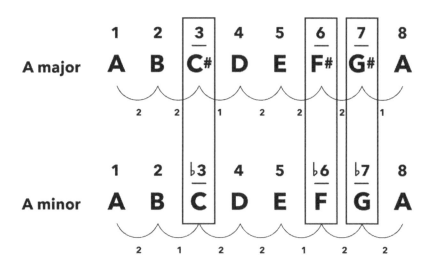

As all major scales have the same formula, and all natural minor scales have the same formula, the differences we have found between A major and A minor are the same for every major and natural minor scale. We can conclude by saying the spelling of all natural minor scales is: 1 2 ♭3 4 5 ♭6 ♭7 8, where the flats tell us that those notes are one semitone down from where they are in major scales. But whyyyyy???

9. DIFFERENCE BETWEEN MAJOR & MINOR TRIADS

Triads are the *simplest chords, as they consist of only three notes*. Chords are built by playing a note in the scale, then skipping over the adjacent note to the right and playing the note above it, and then repeating this play-skip pattern until you have the desired chord.

The first triad in A major is A C# E (known as the A major triad), which sounds happy.
The first triad in A minor is A C E (known as the A minor triad), which sounds sad.

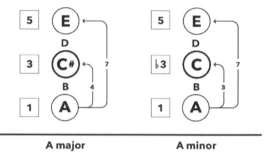

A major   **A minor**

Figure 9.1 Comparison of A major triad to A minor triad

Only one note is different from the A major triad to the A minor triad, the 3rd, yet the emotions are opposite. This reveals that the **third note**, or **3rd**, is the *magic ingredient in music that gives chords and scales their happy or sad sound*.

The 3rd in a minor triad is closer to the root (three semitones) and therefore less harmonious, causing a **dissonant** or *clashing sound* and emotion. The 3rd in a major triad is further away from the root (four semitones) and therefore vibrates more harmoniously, causing a **consonant** or *pleasing sound* and emotion.

The note that completes these triads is called the perfect 5th, due to its perfect mathematical ratio to the root. By the way, the same is true about the octave, which is why it's also referred to as the perfect 8th.

INTERVALS
Minor 3rd (spelling = ♭3) three semitones

Major 3rd (spelling = 3) four semitones
Perfect 5th (spelling = 5) seven semitones
Octave / perfect 8th (spelling = 8) twelve semitones

Okay, okay, I can hear your inner why-kid loud and clear: "I understand the difference between major and minor scales now, but why does the one make me feel happy and the other sad?" Amazing question, and one of the most fascinating musical topics ever. Until recently we battled between the classic nature/nurture divide. Cultural conditioning has certainly deepened this phenomenon. For example, every year when we celebrate being one year wiser, we sing "Happy Birthday" – which is in a major scale – thus reinforcing our association of major scales with happiness. However, in 2009 the isolated Mafa tribe of Cameroon and Nigeria, who'd never been exposed to any music outside of their rural community, were involved in a historic study to find out if they also felt major as happy and minor as sad. They did! The Mafa people ended this debate by evidencing a non-cultural human response to music. This is due to the sound waves vibrating more harmoniously in majors than in minors, proving that we truly are all hardwired to feel music as a universal language – genres are merely dialects.

Let's explore this starting with **triads**, the simplest chords we have. These consist of only three notes. We build chords by playing a note from the scale, then leapfrogging a couple of times. In other words, you play a note in the scale, then skip over the adjacent note to the right and play the note above it, repeating this play-skip pattern until you have the desired chord. We can actually do this through the entire scale until we have all of its notes in our chord, resulting in jazz* – oops, sorry! I mean, resulting in a seven-note chord – but the most common type of chord in popular music is the three-note triad.

When you assemble a triad from the root in A major, you end up with the notes A C♯ E, which is known, unsurprisingly, as the A major triad. When we do the same from the root in A minor, we get the notes A C E, known as the A minor triad. If you play these notes on a piano or bagpipes or whatever instrument you have handy, you'll hear and feel very clearly that the A major triad is exuding happiness into the atmosphere, while the A minor triad gently weeps on our shoulders.

*Oh come now, it was just a little joke. I'm a massive jazz fan, so don't send me hate mail, mmmkay?

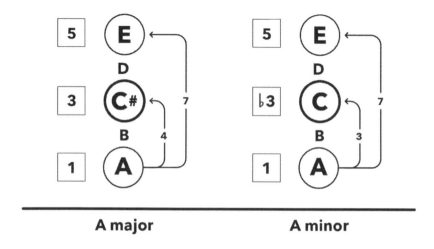

A major   **A minor**

What the hell kind of sorcery is at work here? Only one note is different from the A major triad to the A minor triad, yet the emotions are opposite. This discovery you have just made is profound: the **third note, or 3rd,** is the *magic ingredient in music that gives chords and scales their happy or sad sound.* We could sit around all day drinking tea and chatting about the importance of the 3rd, and that still wouldn't do justice to its utmost gravity. It is impossible to over-emphasise the powers of the happy 3 and the sad ♭3. The interval of *three semitones* is known as the **minor 3rd (spelling = ♭3),** as it's the 3rd note in the minor scale, and the interval of *four semitones* is the **major 3rd (spelling = 3),** because it's the 3rd rung of the major scale ladder. Finally, the note that completes the triad is known as the **perfect 5th (spelling = 5),** due to the perfect mathematical ratio (3:2) of its relationship to the root, which is *seven semitones* away. This means that for every three sound wave vibrations of the perfect 5th, the root vibrates twice. By the way, the same is true about the octave, also known as the **perfect 8th (spelling = 8),** as its notes are *twelve semitones* apart and result in another perfect ratio (2:1).

Finally, why do majors sound happy and minors sad? The root (A in the above example) is our foundation on which the chord is built, so we hear it as the most important note. Minor chords, with the ♭3 (C above) being only three semitones above the root, stir **dissonance** within us from the *clashing sound* of closer note vibrations. Major chords, with the 3 (C♯ above) that's four semitones above the root, resonate with our inner **consonance** to create a *pleasing sound,* thanks to their more spacious note vibrations.

10. SEVEN TRIADS

Major and minor scales have seven notes, and seven notes mean seven triads, one triad starting from each note in the scale. Therefore, every scale has a family of seven triads living within it, and as long as we stick (for now) with these seven triads when we're making music, it will always sound good.

The first triad we get in any key is known as the **root triad**: a triad *built on the first note of a scale*. Then we repeat the play-skip-play-skip-play triad building formula from each of the other notes to uncover the remaining triads in that key.

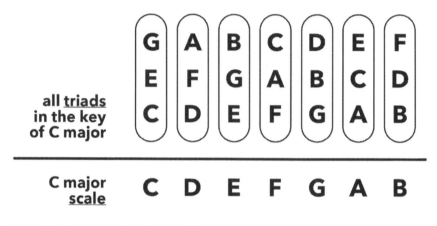

Figure 10.1 All seven triads in the key of C major

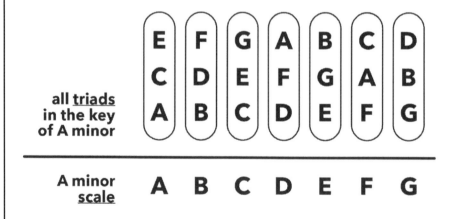

Figure 10.2 All seven triads in the key of A minor

Up until the early 1400s, the only harmony you'd hear would be the colourless perfect intervals: octaves, 5ths, and 4ths. Interesting side note: when two notes an octave apart are played together, many non-musicians hear them as one note. This often occurs with 5ths as well, and sometimes even with 4ths. Perfect intervals vibrate far too similarly to each other, and therefore our ears struggle to differentiate between them.

Six centuries ago, along came the mad scientist genius John Dunstaple. Okay, he wasn't really mad and he wasn't really a scientist either: he was a composer and astrologer. But he was definitely a genius. And yes, this is the same John Dunstaple we met in chapter 3. No exaggeration, J.D. changed music forever. Bear in mind that coming straight out of centuries of perfect intervals, his never-before-heard magic 3rds sounded way more intense than they do now. Play your mum or your nan some proper metal – maybe a little Emperor – and I reckon they'd react kinda like the people did six hundred years ago upon first hearing triads. Extreme!

Onto the practical use of this newfound wizardry. You already know that the major and minor scales have seven notes, so how many triads can we build from each scale? Yep, *seven notes* mean *seven triads*, one triad starting from each note. Let's take things back to C major, the only major scale with no key signature, so that we can work exclusively with the white notes, which is ideal for visualising intervals. The first triad we get in the key of C major is: C E G. This is known as the **root triad**, as it is *built on the first note in the scale*. If we do this same formula again from the second note in the scale, we get the second triad found in the key of C major: D F A. Then the same again from the third note, giving us the third triad of E G B, and so on. Here are all seven:

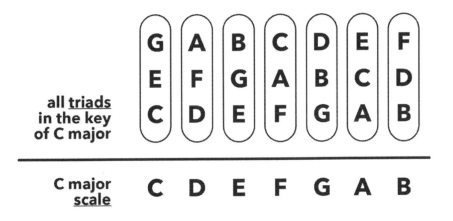

45

Below are all seven triads in the key of A minor, found using the same process as above:

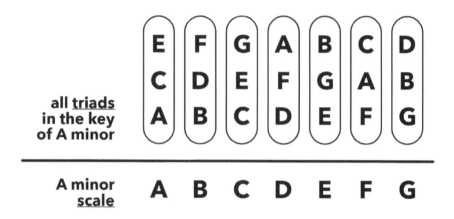

Every scale has a family of seven triads living within it, and as long as you stick with these seven triads when you're making music, it will sound good. We can and will learn about using friend chords that are not represented here, but for now, let's keep it in the family, as that's the safest way to start your musical journey.

11. TRIADS IN MAJOR KEYS

All major keys always have *four minor triads* and only *three major triads* (out of seven triads total), which means that in a major key there are more minor triads than major triads. In other words, in the 'happy' key there are actually more 'sad' chords than 'happy' chords.

This emotional complexity allows us to express sadness within a happy home, and it's how we make music tell the true story of our complex feelings. When we compose a **chord progression** (i.e. *the chords you string together to tell your musical story*), we can eloquently communicate our inner narrative both by the chords we select and by their order.

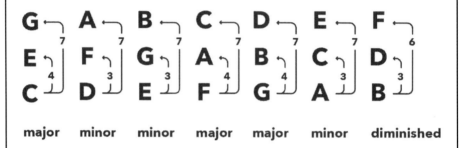

Figure 11.1 The seven triads in all major keys

The **diminished triad** is a *special type of minor triad*, and you can think of it as the black sheep of our family. The three semitones (minor 3rd) between its bottom and middle notes make it a minor, but the six semitone interval (instead of seven semitones) between its bottom and top notes is a diminished 5th,* making it a diminished triad.

INTERVAL
Diminished 5th (spelling = ♭5) six semitones

---

*The diminished 5th is sometimes referred to as a **tritone**. 'Tri' means three, and a 'tone' is two semitones, describing its six semitones (3 x 2 semitones). In medieval Europe this dissonant interval was named the **devil in music** and subsequently banned.

You know that majors lift our spirits while minors drop the tears. So if we play in a major key then it's all happy days, right? Nope, don't judge a book by the cover (well, other than this book, which has an awesome cover *and* awesome content!). Life is not only black and white or happy and sad: it is emotionally complex, and music can reflect that. Yes, of course, major triads are always happy. However, in the key of C major, count the semitones between D F A (the second triad). D to F is three semitones, which is a minor 3rd. What the...?! Oh yes you did! You just found a minor triad in a major key. And you know what, there's more. Count the semitones between the bottom and middle notes in the other triads, and you'll discover something even stranger. E to G, A to C, and B to D are all three semitones as well, making them minors too. That's four minor triads in a major key, and there's only seven triads, which means there are only three major triads in a major key. This is massive news: *There are more minor triads than major triads in a major key.*

This is how we make music tell the true story of our feelings. For example, if you're about to move to another city to pursue an exciting opportunity and you're feeling positive, then chose a major key to convey this. But, as it's a bittersweet move since you have to say goodbye to friends and family, include some minor triads in your sequence of chords, or **chord progression** (i.e. *the chords you string together to tell your musical story*). On the other hand, if you've just broken up with your partner, choose a minor key for your chord progression, but if splitting was the best thing for both of you and you're finally feeling content, add in some major triads to communicate this.

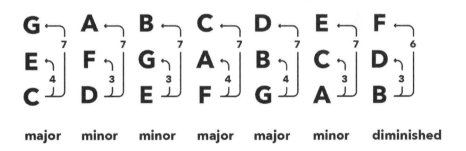

Dim... what!? Let me explain. First, don't stress: there are still four minor triads in every key. The diminished triad is a special type of minor triad: the black sheep of our family. You can see it's minor from the three semitones between its bottom and middle notes, which make it a minor 3rd. Why the weird name then? If you compare its top note to the other triads in the key, you'll notice it only has six semitones instead of the usual seven. You've already learned the interval of seven semitones is a perfect 5th (spelling = 5), and because six semitones is less (i.e. diminished) we refer to the *dissonant interval of six semitones* as a **diminished 5th (spelling = ♭5)**. To conclude, a **diminished triad** has a *minor 3rd (three semitones) and a diminished 5th (six semitones) above its root.*

You'll sometimes hear fellow musicians talking about a **tritone**. That's just another name for the ♭5. 'Tri' means three, and 'tone' means two semitones, so it's describing the six (3 x 2) semitones. Tritone isn't a great name, though, as it doesn't provide the context the way that 'diminished 5th' does, because you know we're talking about the 5th note. For this reason, we won't use the tritone name, but since you might hear it around, you're now in the know. By the way, there's also an enharmonic name for this interval, but we'll get to that later.

The ♭5 is our most infamous interval, with a dark history that stretches back at least a thousand years. You may have heard of the **devil in music**, or, in its original Latin, *diabolus in musica*. That was a rather unflattering name (probably coined by the Roman Catholic Church) used back in the medieval era for the ♭5. To be fair, it is an evil sounding interval, and if you think back to a time when people believed disease was punishment from a god, it's easy to understand why they thought the awful clashing sound from a ♭5 was the devil manifesting himself through music. So there you have it, you've been warned. Use the ♭5 at your own risk!

12. TRIADS IN MINOR KEYS

Major and natural minor scales are relatives of each other, which means that all major and natural minor keys always have *three major triads* and *four minor triads* (one minor triad being the diminished 'black sheep').

By starting on (or emphasising) the 6th triad in a major key, you get the triads in a minor key: minor, diminished, major, minor, minor, major, major.

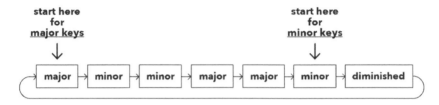

Figure 12.1 The one sequence of seven triads for all major and natural minor keys

A triad can be either *major, minor, or diminished*. This is known as its **chord quality**.

Each of the seven triads has their own root note (i.e. the triad's first note). However, the key itself also has a root note, which is known as the **key-note** (i.e. *the scale's first note*)

TRIADS
Major triad   *triad consisting of a major 3rd (four semitones) and a perfect 5th (seven semitones) above its root*
Minor triad   *triad consisting of a minor 3rd (three semitones) and a perfect 5th (seven semitones) above its root*
Diminished triad   *special type of minor triad, consisting of a minor 3rd (three semitones) and a diminished 5th (six semitones) above its root*

Now, based on your understanding of relative keys and how they're identical twins with opposite personalities (depending on what note you emphasize as the root), you can conclude that all minor keys must also have three major triads, three minor triads, and one black-sheep diminished triad. As we discovered in chapter 5, if you're playing a major scale you can just start on the 6th note and, voilà! You're magically transported into the relative minor scale without changing a note. It's that easy for triads too. Start on the 6th triad in a major key and you've got the triads of a minor key. You only ever have to remember one sequence of seven triads, and that will give you all the answers. To be honest, it won't give you the answer to the ultimate question of what the meaning of life is, but that's an easy one: be kind and make the world a better place by sharing your unique talents! Okay, now that the meaning of life is sorted, we can get back to triads.

Below is the never-changing cyclic sequence of triads in both major and natural minor keys. When you *start on the 6th triad* you get the sequence for *natural minor keys*: minor, diminished, major, minor, minor, major, major.

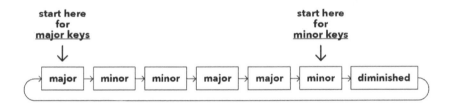

In our music lingo, we refer to a triad being *major, minor, or diminished* as its **chord quality**. When you're making music and you come up with an amazing chord progression, remember to write down the chord qualities of the triads too – not just their roots. There's a super quick and easy way of doing this, which we'll get to in the next chapter.

After reading the above paragraph, you may be wondering about my use of the plural 'roots.' How can a chord progression have more than one root when it's only in one key? Every key contains seven triads, which all have their own roots (i.e. each triad's first note). However, the key itself also has a root (i.e. the scale's first note). Now you're probably thinking that's pretty confusing, and you're right. So, the music gods provided us with a simple solution. Well, it was actually a dead dude, but still, great solution. As I was saying, the simple way to avoid confusion in these situations is to refer to the *root note of a scale or key* as the **key-note**. For example, in the key of A minor, A is the key-note. The second triad in that key is B diminished, so B is the root of that triad, but the overall key-note throughout is always A, because we're in the key of A minor.

Sometimes our musical journeys happen backwards and we start at the destination. This can occur when we're working with someone else and they perhaps use a chord they can't identify, or if we're having a solo jam and stumble across a group of notes that sound cool together. We then have to reverse-engineer that chord without knowing the key or anything else. This is done by first analysing the notes and then placing them in the standard leapfrog order (i.e. play-skip-play – see chapter 9 for more), which also reveals the root. For example, the notes E C A need to be re-arranged into their original leapfrogging order: A C E. Any other way isn't the original form of that chord, such as C E A, as we'd be skipping two notes between E and A. Now we can analyse the intervals by counting their semitones. **Major triads** always contain the semitone pattern of *four and seven above their roots*, while **minor triads** are always *three and seven above their roots*, and, finally, diminished triads are always *three and six above their roots*. Always!

13. CHORD SYMBOLS

Chord symbols are the *quickest and easiest way to notate or document a chord*, which ensures that you can remember it in the future. Chord symbols consist of the *root note* (e.g. C) and *chord quality* (e.g. major). The quality is then abbreviated to **maj** (for major), **m** (for minor), and **dim** or ° (for diminished). Please note, it's always taken for granted that chords are major unless otherwise stated, so a C major triad can be notated as just C – although Cmaj is clearer and therefore preferred.

Spelling-based chord symbols of 'classical' music	Root-based chord symbols of 'popular' music	Hybrid chord symbols (best of both worlds)
I (upper-case for major chords)	Cmaj (or) C	Imaj
ii (lower-case for minor chords)	Dm	IIm
iii	Em	IIIm
IV	Fmaj (or) F	IVmaj
V	Gmaj (or) G	Vmaj
vi	Am	VIm
vii°	Bdim (or) B°	VIIdim

Figure 13.1 The three different approaches to chord symbols, using the key of C major

Spelling-based chord symbols of 'classical' music	Root-based chord symbols of 'popular' music	Hybrid chord symbols (best of both worlds)
i	Am	Im
ii°	Bdim (or) B°	IIdim
III	Cmaj (or) C	♭IIImaj (triad from ♭3 in scale)
iv	Dm	IVm
v	Em	Vm
VI	Fmaj (or) F	♭VImaj (triad from ♭6 in scale)
VII	Gmaj (or) G	♭VIImaj (triad from ♭7 in scale)

Figure 13.2 The three different approaches to chord symbols, using the key of A minor

The compromise with using the extremely concise notation of chord symbols, is that they don't tell us where the notes should be played, but only what the notes are. The only way to notate with 100% accuracy is to use the old-school stave (or new-school MIDI), which we'll cover later in the book series. However, you don't actually need to know any notation at all in order to make music, as notation is merely a way of documenting what you've made.

Remember back in 1992 when Prince (RIP) released that album with the symbol on the cover and it became known as the Love Symbol, and then he started being referred to as "The Artist Formerly Known as Prince"? Yeah, that was pretty cool, but I think you'll find chord symbols to be even cooler. And no diss to the Prince, but chord symbols are also way more useful than love symbols. I'm not going to lie though, we're kind of in a chord symbol limbo right now, stuck between the old 'classical' and new 'popular' worlds, resulting in more variations than you can shake a drumstick at. I'll share with you these two different approaches, as any variation you come across will be based on one of these, or on both, like the new hybrid chord symbol that is being used by the London College of Music.

So, what are chord symbols? They're the quickest and easiest way to notate or document chords, ensuring that you can remember them in the future. Amazing, right? **Chord symbols** are small yet potent doses of musical information, consisting of the *root note* (e.g. C) and the *chord quality* (e.g. major). The quality is then abbreviated to **maj** (for major), **m** (for minor), and **dim** or ° (for diminished). As if that's not concise enough, it's always taken for granted that chords are major unless otherwise stated, which means a C major triad can be notated as just C. (Note: I reckon if you haven't got time to write 'maj' then you don't have time to read this book, so, dear reader, please write out 'maj' as it creates consistency and destroys confusion.) And that's all there is to chord symbols – it really doesn't get quicker or easier than that.

Now onto the 'but' – and you knew there had to be a big butt* with something this good. The compromise for using this concise method is that chord symbols don't tell you where the notes should be played, but only what the notes are. For example, if someone is playing your song from chord symbols, it won't sound exactly the same as how you composed it. It'll sound close to your original as the chords will all be the same, but the notes will be in different positions. The only way to notate with 100% accuracy is to use those old-school five lines (i.e. the stave). It's actually really easy to learn and we'll get to that later in the series, if you're interested. And if you don't want to spend your time drawing little circles on little lines, hey, I totally understand. The good news is that thanks to MIDI technology, those old-fashioned circles and lines are no longer necessary for composing or notating. Yay!

---

*I wonder if this is the first music theory book to have a 'big butt' in it? I really hope so! My parents must be so proud.

The table below demonstrates the three different approaches to chord symbols, using the key of C major:

Spelling-based chord symbols of 'classical' music	Root-based chord symbols of 'popular' music	Hybrid chord symbols (best of both worlds)
I (upper-case for major chords)	Cmaj (or) C	Imaj
ii (lower-case for minor chords)	Dm	IIm
iii	Em	IIIm
IV	Fmaj (or) F	IVmaj
V	Gmaj (or) G	Vmaj
vi	Am	VIm
vii°	Bdim (or) B°	VIIdim

Pros of using spelling: Easy to move songs' chords into other keys (good for accommodating a singer's range).

Cons of using spelling: Hard to decipher Roman numerals and the associated key and chord qualities.

Pros of using roots: Easy to see where and what the chords are, without needing to know the overall key.

Cons of using roots: Hard to move songs' chords into other keys (bad for accommodating a singer's range).

GOODBYE

Woohoo!!! Congratulations, I am beyond proud of you for staying the course through Part 1 of my *Hack Music Theory* book series. You have now graduated from the first level of MSOL (Music for Speakers of Other Languages)! Okay, I just made that up, but the other bit is true: you've reached what I call the foundation stage of music theory. You're now empowered to understand and use the basics of your new language to appreciate what's going on in your favourite songs and, most importantly, to liberate your imagination and start making your own music. Yes, of course, there's still a lot to learn, but it will all be built on this foundation you have so solidly laid.

As you now know, western music consists of a mere twelve notes, and we usually only use seven of them at a time. These seven-note groups are our scales and form the basis of all our music. Scales are our musical menu, and like my favourite Chinese vegan restaurant downtown, Lotus Pond, where I order by number, you also order by number in Restaurant de la Musique (it sounds way fancier in French, doesn't it?). Perhaps it's a gorgeous summer evening and you're in the mood for something light and sweet, so you tuck into a harmonious buffet of 1 3 5 succulent salads that are deliciously uplifting. To complement your dinner, you grab a melodious mix of 2 7 5 6 freshly-squeezed drinks, which you sip one at a time. This major feast of delights is completely customised, ordered by you for you. Nobody else in the restaurant is eating the exact same meal as you, even though they're all ordering from the same musical menu. There are unlimited combinations of yumminess, as is evident from over half a millennium of music all pretty much ordered from the same menu. So sit down, order a combo meal and drinks, see if you enjoy them, and then do it all again. And again. And again. It's not about coming up with the perfect musical meal, it's about trying everything and finding your own unique preferences, which ironically will probably change as soon as you find 'em!

Please remember, perfection is rather easy to achieve when you make music using theory, but perfection is never the goal. Perfection is usually thought of as the quality of being free from flaws, and understanding the language of music (music theory) will ensure you always compose flawless music – that is, musical words with correct spelling, musical sentences with good grammar, musical paragraphs with thoughtful structure, and musical essays with coherency. However, music is a science *and* an art. Science is theoretical, but art is creative. It won't take very long for you to master the scientific side, as you're only ever working with twelve elements. However, the musical stories you can tell with them are truly infinite.

Last, please remember this too. Music theory forms a multi-layered protective bubble around music makers, which gives us confidence in knowing that our music is perfectly composed, while also accepting that people's opinions of our music are purely subjective and based on personal taste. Therefore, forming your protective bubble is arguably the most valuable investment you can make as a musician. It allows us to truly have fun creating and sharing our music, without any stress, self-doubt, or the need for validation. Your bubble may only be one layer thick at the moment, but that's enough for you to safely commence your musical journey. Go forth and compose, my fellow bubble buddy, and I'll see you in the second book of the series where we'll add your second protective layer!

Musica longa, vita brevis.

TEST

Section 1: Scales

Q1. The enharmonic of D♯ is:

_____

Q2. The enharmonic of G♭ is:

_____

Q3. Write one octave of the E major scale:

_____

Q4. Write one octave of the D♭ major scale:

_____

Q5. Write one octave of the G natural minor scale:

_____

Q6. Write one octave of the F♯ natural minor scale:

_____

Q7. What is B ♭ major's relative minor scale?

_____

Q8. What is E natural minor's relative major scale?

_____

Q9. Which scale has the following scale spelling: 1 2 3 4 5 6 7 8?

_____

Q10. Write the scale spelling of the natural minor scale:

_____

Section 2: Chords

Q1. Write the notes of the E ♭ major triad:

_____

Q2. Write the notes of the B major triad:

_____

Q3. Write the notes of the B minor triad:

_____

Q4. Write the notes of the F minor triad:

_____

Q5. Name the following triad: G ♭ B ♭ D ♭

_____

Q6. Name the following triad: E G B

_____

Q7. What is the interval between the root note and the note C in the A ♭ maj triad?

_____

Q8. What is the interval between the root note and the note D in the G ♯ dim triad?

_____

Q9. Using chord symbols, write the triads that are built from each degree of the F major scale:

_____

Q10. Using chord symbols, write the triads that are built from each degree of the E natural minor scale:

_____

ANSWERS

Section 1: Scales

A1. E ♭

A2. F♯

A3. E F♯ G♯ A B C♯ D♯ E

A4. D ♭ E ♭ F G ♭ A ♭ B ♭ C D ♭

A5. G A B ♭ C D E ♭ F G

A6. F♯ G♯ A B C♯ D E F♯

A7. G minor

A8. G major

A9. the major scale

A10. 1 2 ♭3 4 5 ♭6 ♭7 8

Section 2: Chords

A1. E♭ G B♭

A2. B D♯ F♯

A3. B D F♯

A4. F A♭ C

A5. G♭ major triad

A6. E minor triad

A7. major 3rd

A8. diminished 5th

A9. Fmaj Gm Am B♭maj Cmaj Dm Edim

A10. Em F♯dim Gmaj Am Bm Cmaj Dmaj

GLOSSARY

chord three or more notes sounded together (e.g. C E G)

chord progression sequence of chords (i.e. the chords you string together to tell your musical story)

chord quality / quality whether a chord is major, minor, or diminished (e.g. Cmaj has a 'major' quality)

chord symbol quickest and easiest way to notate a chord, using root note and chord quality (e.g. Cmaj)

consonant / consonance pleasing sound (e.g. perfect 5th)

devil in music / *diabolus in musica* old-fashioned name for the diminished 5th, probably coined by the Roman Catholic Church

dim / ° abbreviation for diminished triad, used in chord symbols (e.g. Bdim / B°)

diminished 5th / tritone (spelling = ♭5) dissonant interval of six semitones

diminished triad special type of minor triad, consisting of a minor 3rd (three semitones) and a diminished 5th (six semitones) above its root (e.g. B D F)

dissonant / dissonance clashing sound (e.g. diminished 5th)

enharmonic different name for the same note (e.g. C♯ and D♭)

equal temperament tuning system that divides the octave into twelve equal steps (i.e. semitones)

flat / ♭ one semitone down (e.g. D♭ is one semitone down from D)

harmonic series series of higher notes that are set off from the vibrations of a single note

harmony two or more notes sounded together (i.e. vertical music)

interval space between any two notes, measured in semitones (e.g. twelve semitones is the interval of an octave)

just intonation original 'pure' tuning system that uses whole-number ratios, and works only from one fundamental note at a time

key scale in use (e.g. a melody in the A minor scale is in the key of A minor)
key-note root note of a scale or key (i.e. the scale's first note)
key signature sharps or flats in a scale (e.g. F♯ and C♯ in D major)

m abbreviation for minor triad, used in chord symbols (e.g. Am)
maj abbreviation for major triad, used in chord symbols (e.g. Cmaj)
major 3rd (spelling = 3) interval of four semitones
major scale 'happy scale' made from this semitone formula: *2 2 1 2 2 2 1*
major triad triad consisting of a major 3rd (four semitones) and a perfect 5th (seven semitones) above its root (e.g. C E G)
melody sequence of notes sounded one at a time (i.e. horizontal music)
minor 3rd (spelling = ♭3) interval of three semitones
minor scale / natural minor scale 'sad scale' made from this semitone formula: *2 1 2 2 1 2 2*
minor triad triad consisting of a minor 3rd (three semitones) and a perfect 5th (seven semitones) above its root (e.g. A C E)

naturals white notes on piano (i.e. not a sharp or flat)
natural minor scale / minor scale 'sad scale' made from this semitone formula: *2 1 2 2 1 2 2*
note frequency of vibrations, resulting in the highness or lowness of a sound, aka a pitch (e.g. C)

octave / perfect 8th (spelling = 8) interval of twelve semitones (i.e. same note, but a higher or lower pitched version)
overtones quieter notes that occur in the harmonic series

perfect 5th (spelling = 5) interval of seven semitones
perfect 8th / octave (spelling = 8) interval of twelve semitones (i.e. same note, but a higher or lower pitched version)

pitch frequency of vibrations, resulting in the highness or lowness of a sound, aka a note (e.g. C)

relative major the scale you get when you start on the 3rd note of a minor scale
relative minor the scale you get when you start on the 6th note of a major scale
relatives / relative scale scales that have the same notes, but a different root (e.g. C major and A minor)
rhythm pattern in time (e.g. ta ti-ti ta ta)
root / root note first note of a scale or chord (e.g. D is the root in D major)
root triad triad built on the first note of a scale

scale family of notes that work together
semitone smallest interval in western music and is an interval of one step (e.g. C to C♯)
sharp / ♯ one semitone up (e.g. C♯ is one semitone up from C)
spelling numerical way of writing music (e.g. major scale = 1 2 3 4 5 6 7 8)
step semitone ('step' is not a musical term, and is therefore ambiguous)

tempo speed at which music is played (e.g. 120 BPM or beats per minute)
third note / 3rd magic ingredient in music that gives chords and scales their happy or sad sound
tone / whole tone interval of two semitones (e.g. C to D)
tonic first note of a scale (e.g. D is the tonic in D major)
triad simplest chord, consisting of only three notes (e.g. 1 3 5)
tritone / diminished 5th (spelling = ♭5) dissonant interval of six semitones

whole tone / tone interval of two semitones (e.g. C to D)

ACKNOWLEDGMENTS

My major 3rd, Kate Harmony, without whom I am a mere root. My blood fam: Mumsta, Pops, Tony aka T-bone, Granny T, Gramps RIP (my ol' birthday buddy and inspiration), and all the rest of ya. The mighty Susan Church and my adopted Haddow clan. My main man Rob Krammer. My A-Team: Kendra Marks, Maria Picassó, and Shawn S. Mihalik. The lovely people who said lovely things about this here strange book of mine: Derek Sivers, Ihsahn, Dr Vicky Williamson, Joe Copcutt, and Pat Lundy. Drew Betts aka Vespers for believing in me and my weird ideas. Greg Barker for igniting the publishing spark in my mind. Laura Lang for supporting my vision. My beta testers, Andrew Dunn and Lena Goodfellow. Damn, thank you lists are difficult, as I basically wanna thank everyone. Can I do that? Is that a thing? Oh yeah, it's my book, I can do whatever I want. Ahem. C, E ♭ and G walk into a bar. Barman says: "Sorry, we don't serve minors". Ba-dum-bum-ching! Fine, don't laugh then, I thought it was pretty funny, and I don't even drink. Still, it's awesome you get that joke now, right? And, while we're on the subject of how awesome you are, thank you for having the courage to follow your musical dream and to do it properly, through education. It's an honour to be a part of that. Also, thanks a bunch for spending your hard-earned cash money on my book – that means the world to me. And finally, thank you to everyone who has ever helped me in any way, shape, or form, I remember you and I am grateful. Thank you :)

BORING STUFF & COOL PEEPS

REVOLUTION HARMONY

Editing by the amazingly amazing Kendra Marks
Cover art, design, and diagrams by the genius Maria Picassó
Formatting and text design by the legendary Shawn S. Mihalik
Guidance, proofreading, and everything else by my favourite singer, Kate Harmony
Additional proofreading by word-detective Alyson Fortowsky
Photography by camera ninja Billie Woods

Library and Archives Canada Cataloguing in Publication

Harmony, Ray, author
Hack Music Theory, Part 1: Learn Scales & Chords in 30 Minutes / Ray Harmony.

1. Music Theory. 2. Composing. 3. Songwriting. I. Title.

ISBN 978-1-988410-00-5 (paperback)
ISBN 978-1-988410-01-2 (pdf)
ISBN 978-1-988410-02-9 (epub)
ISBN 978-1-988410-03-6 (mobi)

RevolutionHarmony.org